Absence has a weight
of its own

Absence has a weight of its own

Daniel Sluman

ISBN: 978-0-9570984-6-6

Scan QR code for further title information

First published June 2012 by:

Nine Arches Press
Great Central Studios
92 Lower Hillmorton Rd
Rugby
Warwickshire
CV21 3TF

www.ninearchespress.com

Printed in Britain by:

imprintdigital.net
Seychelles Farm,
Upton Pyne,
Exeter
EX5 5HY
www.imprintdigital.net

Absence has a weight of its own

Daniel Sluman

Nine
Arches
Press

new poets series

Daniel Sluman is a 25 year old Postgraduate studying Creative and Critical Writing at the University Of Gloucestershire. He has been published widely in journals such as *Popshot, Shit Creek Review & Orbis.* He is currently on the editorial board for the journal *Iota. Absence has a weight of its own* is his first collection of poems.

CONTENTS

THREE

For Sonia and Harrison

ABSENCE

Gas flooded lungs tense;
turned spluttering breath
to moth-balled lips
as they cleaved me at the hip;
the flesh was stitched taut,
a finer fabric tore.

Unlike the gold rush of cancer
it entered slowly; grew fat
in my pulse — the tick in my wrist
as I slid through a classroom,
its face swept in hair
that bled to the floor,

that smile
ripping a knife
through the linen
of my childhood; saying
'absence has a weight of its own'.

ONE

ROMAN & DETERMINISM

He takes me outside
into the whore-soaked night,

cold enough to split us open

like bags of confetti. Sidling me
into a stall at the bar, he claims

we're walking narratives.

The jetstream of each decision
glitters for a second in the air

like the wake of an argument.

FIRST

Like breaking
the spine of a book;

the vanilla scent
before the thumb-marks

& spider-trailed notes
wedged in the margins.

We fumbled at each other
like that moment in *Wizard Of Oz,*

when everyone's eyes strained
from white to bleeding tongues of colour.

Summer at the Farm

Our throats burnt with sherbet
& *fuck* rattled our tongues lazy
as we tore at strawberries,

our fingers smacking
at the lesson in life cycles;
raspberries throbbing to thumbs,

or that afternoon we watched
Wendy's blood wisp, bloom ringlets
on the white of her thighs.

We slept to fireflies
humming stubble on our cheeks,
the night twitching in our dreams

of poolsides, strapless bras,
the seeds in our heads ticking
against the salt in our blood.

Radiance

Their lips & fingers fuse for a second,

the breeze catching split-ends mid-air
as rain frames their tumbled posture,

until clouds smooth tracing paper

over the moon. They pull apart
but waiver like magnets

too-close together,

turning their backs, propelled
by the empty-palmed wind to estates

where roads writhe in endless cul-de-sac.

LORNE ROAD

Big Mac wrappers haunt the air
as I step outside on the wet pavement

stubbled with glass. Tonight we'll be

soothed to sleep with the sound of pints
exploding against the wall. We'll dream

of single mothers defrosting stillborns

in casserole pots; wake to the grand
unveiling of another morning streamed

in the yolk-yellow of police tape.

DREAM

Two pages stuck
between thumb & finger

& no grip, no distance
between the just-gone

& the present; back-alleys
of endless footnotes,

a compass full of north.
Each time your glossia

is frozen, a sheet taut
with premonition, your eyes

are screaming & my hands —
crows tearing an escape route

— until your voice buckles
the night & we wake;

the taste of tomorrow
on the roof of our mouths.

ABANDON

Your body is snapping back into shape,

stomach as smooth as an envelope
as I sleep in my cot, a tiny bomb

fattening with your future. You stretch

your teenage bones over the hospital sheets,
surrounded by the mute applause of Hallmark.

This alimony of feeling won't shake,

you make a choice; there is a sparrow
outside the window, it twitches its head

upwards & whips into the empty sky.

LOVE SONG TO A TUMOUR

When they ripped you from me
I saw a greasy bundle of fireworks,

nature's atom bomb. It's not the impact
which hurts, but the fall-out that settles

like fibreglass in my eyes; I see the entropy
in everything, the date printed in my blood,

a loose thread stitched in the lining of my lungs.
At night we pull the bone-cluttered duvet over us,

our shadows slide like clothes thrown on a lampshade.

LETTER

You may feel like you've drained
all the clock has for you,

but this isn't forever;

your *comingsofage* packed
in ice, each needle smiling

like a lover. When you wake

to find a tube hanging from your chest
your ears will swarm with bees,

the doctor will catch you

just before you hit the tiles.
You will never feel more alive than now:

someone else's blood sizzling

under your skin, your mother's make-up
shaking to the floor. The tumour on the x-ray

tells you life is a fistful of cobwebs.

After the Wedding

Back then, you were *so* London
with your ecstatic white teeth,
guest lists blissed from your fingers
like weather reports.

I have adored your ankles,
snaffled the fine hairs that crisp
the small of your back,
& now, after I've licked

the soap-traces from the underside
of your knees, we find ourselves
stalled in the marriage bed;
your maiden name

a peppercorn crushed
in my mouth. A chandelier
hangs above us, the links of the chain
are tiny & numerous, & if one came loose,

if it bent under the strain,
well, I guess what I'm asking is
where do we go
from here?

OTHER

She is the pin this city heaves upon;

her leg hanging out of the balcony, rain
hissing against her toes as she watches

the pink-smudged skyline engulf the building-tops.

Tonight she'll shave herself to virginity & wash
the appetite from her hair, cramp her head to the pillow

& dream of tearing down houses with her teeth.

WE DAREN'T GO BACK

where the bedroom walls glittered
with premonition, night-sweats starched

sheets bitter; my midnight resurrections
trampled lines as I chased myself

into the mirror, a shaking finger muddying
the bottom of a bag. I could have lost you;

that revelation greasing my hands over
the bright steel sink, splitting capsules

like wafers of bread. You peeled
out my name & floated behind me,

arms crossing my chest, saying
no, that's not what I meant.

GOD

In response to Ros Barber's 'Goddess'.

He will be loud. His tongue trapped
with thunder, the glossy syntax

unreeled to flypaper your dreams.
He will howl you naked, the host

of words sliding from his palm
to your cheek as he kicks

the legs from under you,
cups your light like a lampshade,

your filament rattling alarm
that he'll muffle from the world.

FICTION

There is poetry
in the way his fists glisten
with desire & kiss each notion
from my head like they were slates
of acetate.

If you could see
the magic of his knees
pinning me like a birthday card
between collarbones & shoulders,
pouring whisky in my eyes

from his miraculous distance —
you'd know that I was born
to trip this broken fuse.

He will weld the scattered pages
of my soul together.
He will bind me
into fiction.

YOUR LIMP BREATH SLIDES OFF THE HOSPITAL WALLS

as the nurse tells me how they found you

transfixed under your Ford, spanner-in-hand,
eyes bursting petroleum rainbows. You never excavated

the bodies behind your cracked lexicon of *Normandy,*

Pointe du Hoc. As a child I watched you simmer
in your corner chair, your years melting to corduroy

as fresh blood flickered on the newsreel. We wrap

your history in the headlines of the paper, & I think
of you, sealing yourself in a lead coffin where

the faces of the men you shot burst like poppy seeds.

LOVE SONG TO A NOTEBOOK

Before the crowds scurry into the arcade
we sit on the bench & plane my week

into neat couplets; the stanza's breathe
too heavy, the dark muscle's

clenched instinct. I try to pay the debts
still spiralling inside me. I have drawn

the silk from crumpled nights, stirred foreign
from miraculous sheets, but nothing looks right

in your balloon-blue sleeve. These similes
are codes to a trick rebuffed fifty years ago;

all writing is a construction of hold-music
& neither of us will wait for the rest of my life.

TWO

Roman's Ghost

She spat it into a plastic cup,
fell back, smearing her lips with her knuckles;
his stomach rolling knots under her head.

He tells her how his father split like a yolk
under his mistress, his mother learnt to change
tyres, measure the life left on a dipstick,

clamp silence. Roman clasps the side
of the girl's face like a just-spun globe;
turns the beaker in his other hand, watching

his spectre congeal, grow, beat
its dumb fists against the side, a continent
muted, screaming nothing but the past.

TRANSCRIPT

There was so much,
         so much red.

Everything   stopped
for a second.

I caught it
       in my eye;

we turned
slowly
     upside
           down
&
  settled,

the windscreen
full of veins.

We started to laugh
as we looked,
thinking

       the metal missed,

but he didn't look right,

staring
at his slick palms

& then shaking one hand
into mine.

I held it as he smiled
but he couldn't

choke the words,
& there were
no words.

Snow/Swinging #2

Still bruising
from the hurricane   of elbows,

the chassis rattled   like a ouija-glass.

We pressed   the horoscopes
for truth, the radio   promised
staggered   fall-out.

Last night left   nothing untouched,
history   licked
from the creases,

now, the trees
by the road
are throttled   with glitter,

the sun   purses the horizon

& the shadows   we nailed
                    to
                                      the floor

start to stir.

PORTRAIT AT A CAFÉ

She tears at the sheets
of her loose-bound notebook
but means to unravel
herself. Her hands

private suicides
stiffening life into ink.
I wince at the force
in her thumb; three divorces

tense the pages into the past.
She sips her cappuccino
& floats back to the evenings
when a single line

would catch, spark,
igniting everything below.
She is gulping down
the months before we met.

PICNIC

You narrowed
on the wrong details;

how her hair trapped
the light or her nails burnt

half-moons into the pale
of your arms. A fistful

of letters & three years
later you can still hear

the slow-scream
of her hymen tearing

through the grass;
how you both shivered

behind the eyes
like pages in the wind.

Ambition & the individual talent

You stare until the letters tremble
like needles on a pine tree.
You can smell god in a line-break,
taste a heart attack in *italics*.

This stiff sea of ink shakes
something loose; optic fires spill
hours into days, ransacked
in an attempt to print a page
that beats in your hand,

that when placed
on the scales
weighs exactly;

miracle.

SCENES FROM A FILM

I construct truth
from the bottom

of a glass as she clamps

her teeth on a straw,
watching the sentences

tumble from my lips.

*

Her breasts slide

along the grain
of the table,

breath splintering

the air like pine
as my thumbs bloom

her hips to purple petals.

*

I have pulled apart
the machinery of that night

for the last ten years,

bones heavy with her name
&, whether she meant
to unpack herself

down the basement
stairs, the crack of her

ankles still flood my dreams,

& death is the most final
display of sincerity.

When our pupils swallowed the irises black

The party was a fist of jazz notes,
all wrong except in context;

fashionistas bashed their fists
to a pulp on the bathroom wall,

love-slashed girls rattled
in the throats of middle-aged men.

This morning we clear the cans that gleamed
neon in the arse-end of the evening,

clutch the red-spittled glasses
that rolled on the floor. Next week

we will have forgotten the motives
that slipped down our throats,

the afterthoughts stiffening in smoke.
We'll return where we left, forgetting

when we started; each breath
binding us tighter to the past.

JIMINY CRICKET

Your feet flutter on the duvet,
fingers scuttling over my greasy brain.

Your whisper is the sound of a blade
scraping my thigh, your throat the long shadow

of Freud, you have grown fat on my indecision,
your eyes — Hiroshimas' bursting their bulbs,

reminding me of the quiet digits I've locked in my phone,
the change I've hushed in the hands of taxi drivers.

THE BARMAID

pours a shot of vodka
to the bottom of an iced glass,
turns, silver nails coaxing

Sambuca & Jack from the air,
the millilitres flowing down
her tattooed arms into tumblers.

I bite the lip over, slip the base in the air
& set it down on the bar like a preface,
make one more order & wake up

to the walls hissing memory;
my slate lungs choking on her
ink-work, how her glass back bowed.

*

Her face is a fracture of angles
under the morning's thud of light;
her cheek pockmarked from three years

of bastards; how her voice fell
four dress sizes, all the dinners deflating
in the oven, waiting for them to come home.

I leave to the first pigeons exhaling
into flight, wings frothed in cloud,
cracking their beaks against the sky.

WHEN LIGHTNING SWITCHBLADES

the sky to ribbons, ripping
the cloud's load onto the street

like hurled copper, you realise

you have spent most of your life
like a dull bird in God's breast-

pocket, staring into space,

waiting for something
to happen. You could tighten

this world in inky loops,

tourniquet this moment
before it bleeds out.

Nostalgia

When the evening
is crepe-paper thin
I reel back those first
salmon-faced attempts;

      the girls' mouths
      clumsy with lipstick
      & vodka, the stutters

under tables
& fumblings in cold
Krakow apartments.

Some have tried
to crease it from my heart,
pooling it to pockets
in their cheeks,

others
untangling
knots of silk
for the sake
of the coffee-meet

reveal.

*

Memory neglects regret;
the small slow death

in each name you've gasped,

hunched spectres you carry
fresh to each bed;

>how their eyes dull
in the mirror
of your face.

THIS IS NOT A DRILL

She thinks she wakes,
  the room choked
    with black swathes,

    starts to dress
  but the cry cracks
    her stomach, her soles

thump the corridor
  to the door creased
    with orange tulips,

    braces her weight
  through the hinges;
    the cot is moving

& she looks inside,
  but it's so curious
    & unexpected

RAIN

For four months

you've been in every storm
I've seen, curved

with the meteorologist's arm
as the clouds finger the border;

the summer's static fuzz
& concrete-coloured downpour.

Each time you've stood staring,

silent as the moment two heads
turn in bed, as ours used to;

ankles linked & our bodies split
symmetric; you facing

the wall, me, the door.

Cocaine Roman

He rubbed his numbed ape-gums
with his index finger & fell

to the lounge with Lisa, her eyelashes
spoking his breath like spider-legs.

Time and lines run away
from themselves;

the Genesis of each eye
blooming black,

the tachycardic heart swelling
veins to chase themselves.

He calls her *mother* by mistake —
I cringe, she doesn't. I'm the ghost

in the corner without pyrotechnics,
watching his nail score the mirror.

He takes me back a year
when that Jeep span like a coin,

spat itself at the barrier
& unloaded on both lanes.

We picked off slivers of steel
for a week, found nails

preserved in the windscreen;
mosquitos in amber.

We traced our fingers
over the obituaries for days.

I resigned over it, like now —
my lips over Lisa's tongue

and then the Shakespearean bed swap;

Roman moving through her
like a swallowed drink,

& I'm left, a passenger.

My death

Outside, rain needles through branches
& it all seems so silly, how we flinch

down this brutal coda. Each night, nurses'
shoes clap linoleum towards dazzling alarms;

they have started smoothing out my organs
one by one, like lights in an office block.

The pills make everything taste like tinfoil.
I'm aware of my breath — the push & pull

of this fine wire; I can't control my spit,
everyone winces from my glistening chin.

When the doctor brought in my scan
my liver had bloomed a Rorschach test,

& we all stared, seeing only one thing.

PARALYSIS

You would come each day,

your eyes over mine,
the slow curdle of your lips

tightening around 'sorry'.

A butterfly pressed between pages;

five years has ached a pirouette
across the corridor, it's been a month

since your last apology.

I am outliving us, memory
a grit in silk sheets, the image

of us drying the North Sea
from our hair ghosts through

my blood, this bouquet of veins

tightens, as each false future
tumbles into the next.

THE BLACK SCREEN

coughs a clutch of pixels that dance

like cancer. Flickers ripple
into synthesis, the angle shifts.

The jury catch the red, streaming

like a party-popper, as shadows
become legs, a triumphant shoal

of steel-capped toes penetrating

the skull, face, a juddering bag
of nerves, the evidence —

a stenographer's march into history.

DEAR SAMARITANS, I'M WRITING THIS TO LET YOU KNOW THAT EVERYTHING'S OKAY NOW

The last time we spoke

I was smearing the red flag
of myself around the tub;

the bottle & knife clinking

in my hand. I mentioned
that since I was a child

I have been narrowing

all the questions in the world
to matchsticks, striking them

against my skull, I don't know
how I felt nothing so utterly.

I've learnt patience,
not everything has to wisp

from my fingers. There is a priest
who prays for me; they fly

off his knuckles & hang in the air,

swooping, their feathers
line my pillow. If he could see

these gaping white smiles

on my arm, could taste
the dreams that split my sleep,

he'd understand. God sees me

as a tiny pink coffin, wandering

from place to place, waiting
to fall into the open earth.

THREE

Roman always spoils it

He carves his way through the crowd;
hair slicked back with the spine of a knife

and reeling a gaggle of short-skirted bobs
with his lighter tricks and stories of Prague.

He shotguns the brunette
with the up-to-the-arse stockings,

nods the chubby blonde my way. I'm left
eyeing her bucket-of-smashed-crabs face

whilst Roman has his girl flicking
tassels off her salmon blouse.

*

The morning unfolds girls walking barefoot
& make-up-less, mascara and memory
tumbled together, tattooed to the pillows.

I cook breakfast for the ten who huddle
around *Hollyoaks*. Roman is long gone,
his aftershave left weaving around the eggs

firming in the pan. As rashers tighten
I can sense the brunette's face slide

across the worktop. I feel her stockings
shiver as Roman eels his way up.

A FIST OF TAXIS ANNOUNCES THAT IT'S 3 AM

The club evaporates;
a cross-stitch of skinny jeans
& throbbing egos swell the lit exit,

but the beat still rips a river under us,
fingers swimming in vodka
& digits exploding

as the understanding of tonight
crawls up my stomach & rolls
over my tongue. My lips open

& you watch them move
& your mouth is parting
as you say yes.

You are saying *yesyesyes*
& you mean it like hell.

THE GRAMMATOLOGIST'S GIRLFRIEND

We tripped over commas all summer,
ampersands bursting your blouse of blasé

American chat. Swinging our keys over the pier,
we bracketed whole topics in the undercurrents

of silence, (lips) slipping assonance, (your fingers)
covered in ink. where I touched you,

& put a full stop where I shouldn't have;
your exclamation marks march!ng down the road.

Holiday

The sun fell, smashing pumpkin
& purple against the edge of the ocean.

We caught its shrapnel in the frame;
your son frozen in the foreground,

packing wet mounds into castles,
his eyes fixed on the present,

his eyes so brown & un-me.
I thought of home, where bulbs

burnt their glass hearts in the night,
where *anniversary* shakes a line

of ink on the calendar. In the shower,
your thighs are oyster-smooth,

head tilted back, hands mangled in hair,
our life resting its weight on the soaped floor.

THE AFTERMATH

Blossoms of cherry tobacco loosen
where you stop mid-arabesque;

wiping the grey pollen of ash
from your skirt, hissing the fag dead

in the damp washing up bowl.

Last night can't escape your kitchen;
late-night Lowell has yellowed

the walls, we draw the blind
to find Paterson's sonnets

fluttering to the floor.

There are the other words too;
the ones we've let slide

down the back of the fridge,
that stain our hands like gunpowder;

sprung down the phone to taxi drivers
or clamped under tongues.

When I get back to my house
a slam of the door sends some Buckley

tumbling; adjectives break in my hands
like your smile — ripping wide as I brush

'Lover, you should've come over'
from my hair.

Kiss

Violins eased from speakers
& hovered around our gestures

as a whole summer bled into that night,
a shoddy polaroid. The air tightened

to a single stitch as I realised you could
burn holes in my stomach, would leave me

wavering over the phone, hurling well-fed
adjectives through the air whilst keeling port

down my throat like a ship in a bottle. Waiting
for the sails to be raised in my ribs, flailing at x.

EPIPHANY

Her skin is a tissue
of quotations, she can lift

Eliot from her arms, her hands

are verbs, adjectives prickle
her palms like rain. Inseparable

from memory & desire, I tried

writing a poem without her,
emptied of breath, the lines

bloomed dust in my throat.

I have picked out our life
to a ghost-rhyme & wrapped

her syllables around my neck,

failing, here, her tiny stilettos
print an ellipsis on the page…

EVOCATION

Her name is a fat fuse
tensed between your teeth,

greased with possibilities

that rise & fall like the pale arc
of her hips. You swallow & she is smoke

easing through your muscles

as you soothe the car to the lights.
At green, the clutch chokes & you sling

past the crossroads like a weight

has evaporated; as if something
was leaning on the brakes

all this time.

SO THIS IS WHAT IT FEELS LIKE

A stranger finds a space on the bench
next to me, blows her nose & sniffs

through a blizzard of Marlboro.
She glances at the litter of ink

in my notebook & turns to her phone.
I look down; keep one eye on the sweep

of her calf, try to picture her arse
slung on the edge of a bed,

my fingers in the smoke of her hair,
but I can't. It's snowing, a girl shakes

in the space next to me. I can't imagine
fucking her, & I realise I'm in love.

E

The opening dissolve
of a home movie;
light glosses the room,

pans to our jaws
magnetised together,

our pupils swell
as serotonin explodes
in the cradle of our stomachs.

We present in the darkness;
two continents, measuring

our borders, dazzled
at each other's fault-lines,
suddenly sensing

why we slip, fall again
and again inside each other;

the feeling, no longer like looking
at your own mortality spill
under a streetlamp.

DEDICATION

'the more I live the more I think
two people together is a miracle'
— Adrienne Rich

Jeff Buckley's soul steams
from the speakers downstairs,

where you hum, shuffling in your slops,

dropping bacon in hot oil, dashing cutlery
on an epiphany of china.

*

My mind settles like a spun coin

warbling to silence. The fresh intimacy
of your sheets is a currency

I'll fritter on cheap flimsy words;

if you cleaved me in two
you'd smell your perfume on my bones.

THIS VIEW

A million people are laying heads

on the tender of their arms, staring
at their lover's back as they sleep,

scrying the sigh of freckles

for points in some irrevocable future;
cut-off phone lines, numbers found

in back-pockets, the history you encase

in cardboard, diluted with each new postcode.
I scan my girlfriend's shoulders for dark-weather,

listening for the folded thunder of a tumour.

I hear the screams of my unborn children,
their blood films my hands. Tonight,

mortgages will swell & plates will loosen

themselves from the wall
as we are buried by the night.

ACKNOWLEDGMENTS

Many thanks to the editors of the following publications, where some of these poems first appeared:

Wordgathering, Snakeskin, The Night Light, Cadaverine, Under The Radar, Clinic, NAWE Young Writer's Hub, Orbis, Ink Sweat & Tears.

I am greatly indebted to Sonia Hendy-Isaac, Nigel McLoughlin, Kate North, Angela France, and Jane Commane. Your proof-reading and support during the writing of this collection has been invaluable. Thanks also go to my family, for supporting me and my decision to come back to University.

Debut
new poets series

Debut is a brand new series of first collections from up-and-coming poets, published by Nine Arches Press. The series represents a selection of the best new voices from the contemporary poetry landscape and work that excites, challenges and provokes its readers.

Since 2008, Nine Arches Press have published over twenty poetry pamphlets and books, including titles which have won the East Midlands Book Award and been chosen as the Poetry Book Society Pamphlet Choice in 2011. As publishers, they are dedicated to the promotion of poetry by both new and established poets, and the development of a loyal readership for poetry. Find out more about Debut and Nine Arches Press by visiting their website at **www.ninearchespress.com** or by scanning this QR Code:

studio harringman

Studio Harringman is a multi-disiplinary creative studio based in East Sussex. For our clients we serve as a complete creative resource; strategy, design and production. We have over 30 years experience in design, branding and advertising. Our client list includes BBC, Thames Television, Universal Pictures, Home Office, Revlon, Warner Brothers, Fremantle and the Shaftesbury Theatre. Run as a family business, the studio was founded by Gary Harringman in 1999 with James Harringman joining the company in 2009. We believe in a world where anyone can publish, quality will always shine through.

www.studioharringman.com